# RESTORING YOUR PEACE
Painful Lessons Learned but Worth the Cost

# RESTORING YOUR PEACE
Painful Lessons Learned but Worth the Cost

## CANDACE PATRICK

**RESTORING YOUR PEACE**
Copyright © 2018 Candace Patrick
All rights reserved.

No part of this book may be reproduced, distributed or transmitted in any form by any means, graphics, electronics, or mechanical, including photocopy, recording, taping, or by any information storage or retrieval system, without permission in writing from the publisher, except in the case of reprints in the context of reviews, quotes, or references.

Unless otherwise indicated, scripture quotations are from the Holy Bible, King James Version. Book Cover Artwork: Madison Williams

All rights reserved.
Printed in the United States of America
ISBN: 978-0-692-11955-6

# Table of Contents

Introduction ................................................................. 1

Chapter 1 – A Giver of Help ........................................ 3

Chapter 2 – From Cancer to Purpose ........................ 7

Chapter 3 – My Marriage Behind a Closed Door .......... 23

Chapter 4 – Don't Take Your Marriage for Granted ....... 39

Chapter 5 – Make Me Over ........................................ 43

Chapter 6 – Forgiving to Have Peace .......................... 55

Chapter 7 – Be Mindful of What You Do .................... 59

Chapter 8 – The Power of God's Grace and Mercy ........ 71

Chapter 9 – I Am Restored with Peace ........................ 83

Restoring Your Peace ................................................. 87

Thank You ................................................................. 89

About the Author ...................................................... 91

# Introduction

Life is a gift; and with this gift comes your ability to make choices that will greatly impact your life. Some of your choices may be positive or negative, but regardless, all will impact your state of mind, the condition of your heart, and the expression of your soul. The negative choices of others or even of yourself can sometimes make you feel like you want to give up on life. However, positive choices can lead to a life of prosperity and peace. Although nothing in life happens by accident, it is up to you to find your purpose.

At times, the storms and challenges that come in our lives are unpredictable. The storms I've gone through in my life had me wondering if my life was going to end. At the age of twenty-six, I became a mother. A year later, I was diagnosed with stage III colon cancer. I was a self-employed cosmetologist with no medical benefits. Soon after my diagnosis, I went from being married to divorced within three years. I faced death, betrayal, infidelity, hopelessness, and anger. My faith was tested, and to get through it, I cried, forgave, loved, supported, and encouraged myself. Most importantly, I prayed for serenity. Every thought, feeling, and loss I experienced did not make sense to me until later.

Through my perseverance and prayers, I survived. Now, I am stronger, wiser, and better.

I am sharing my story with you in hopes that it may offer you comfort, insight, and encouragement to endure whatever storm you may be experiencing. As you read this book, think about the situations and challenges you have endured in your life and consider these questions:

- What are the experiences in my life trying to teach me about myself?
- In what ways do I need to learn to trust in my faith?
- Are there areas in my life where I need to forgive myself or others?

Throughout the book, you will see two categories of reflection:

- **#LessonLearned**, which highlights a key lesson I learned through my experience.

- **#WorthTheCost**, which spotlights the biggest and greatest takeaway from the lesson that has transformed my life.

My prayer is that this book will support you in restoring your peace.

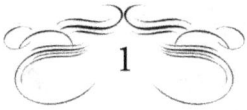

# A Giver of Help

Whenever you feel the divine pull in your heart to give to a person, that is when you should give. You know that this pull is from God because it feels like peace, and you desire nothing in return. Always try to be a giver and helper with a pure heart. Others around you may try to make you feel as if you owe them more by giving. They may feel as if they are entitled to what you offer, or the amount of blessing you may receive should be counted and measured by them somehow and should automatically transfer to them.

Sometimes, I felt like I was helping all of the wrong people because of their poor responses to what I gave. But I learned that no help is wasted in giving from my heart. I have learned more about how people want to be helped instead of deciding for them. Everyone is walking their own journey, has their own experiences in life, and responds to what life brings them in different ways. Those who have wronged you may require your help again; if that happens, guard your heart but always remain genuine.

I am passionate about showing up to help others in challenging situations and leaving that situation in a better state than when I arrived. Despite the challenges I've endured in my life, maintaining this aspect of myself has been constant. I have never wanted to turn cold and stop doing what feels good for me: helping others in their time of need. I have never lost anything by giving or helping someone wholeheartedly because the good deeds you do for others never go unnoticed. It is better to give than to receive, and I enjoy seeing people win in life.

Once, someone who I considered a friend asked me for financial help to achieve a goal. If I helped her, my friend promised to return the loan and let me experience the winning feeling with her once she reached her goal. Prior to my friend asking me for help, I had received an unexpected financial blessing, and God placed it on my heart to help her. I made the sacrifice and I told my friend she did not have to return the loan. After I told her that, she still insisted that she would let me experience the winning feeling with her for going above and beyond, so I accepted what she wanted to do for me in return.

When she won, she did not remain loyal to her word! I was hurt initially, but I was calmed by my upbringing in church, which taught me that when you give, you actually receive. At times, people have mistaken my kindness as a sign that I am weak or gullible, or that I lack self-confidence. However, I view these virtues of kindness and the willingness to help as important strengths that help me endure and overcome other challenges.

---

### #LessonLearned

Do not miss the blessing God has in store for you because of your unwillingness to give others what you have. If I'm not willing to take a loss, then I reconsider whether giving or allowing someone to borrow is good for me at that time. In other words, I don't give unless it comes from my overflow because giving them something I do not have to give in the first place puts me in a place of lack.

---

### #WorthTheCost

I realized that sometimes God will make you bless someone in your circle of friends in order to remove them from your circle. God's favor has become higher on my priority list than recognition, as I've learned that when giving, not everyone who receives will be appreciative. Giving has to be purely from your desire to serve.

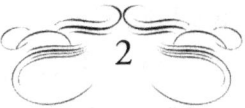

# From Cancer to Purpose

I believe in the power of prayer and that all things are possible. That said, success is not a fairy tale with the perfect journey, and it doesn't happen overnight. When you are trying to become successful, life can treat you unfairly, but your struggles will not last.

Success is not about money; it's about discovering your gift and the purpose of your gift. Discovering your purpose challenges you in ways you may not be prepared for. However, do not let your fears or challenges keep you from going into the unknown, because in doing so, you find success in uncovering your purpose. It is through your willingness to go into the unknown and challenge yourself that you learn more about who you are and what you are capable of. The goal of finding your purpose and gift is in the journey of learning how to focus on becoming a better you for the sake of you only—no one else. If you do not push yourself, you will be stuck in the same place.

Growing up, I always wanted to be a cosmetologist. As a child, I would practice hairstyles on my mother and sisters' hair. During my high school years, I enrolled in a cosmetology program at the Barnwell County Vocational School, and after completing the program, I took the State Board of Cosmetology exam and did not pass it. I passed the second time, two months after I graduated from high school.

In 1999, I became a licensed cosmetologist. I was excited and ready to start my career, until my father said to me, "You need to get a degree because you are going to get tired of standing on your feet all day." Though I didn't agree with him and really wanted to pursue my passion for cosmetology, I enrolled in the University of South Carolina Aiken and majored in math and computer science.

My college years were a struggle. It was hard trying to force myself to be somewhere I did not want to be. I stopped turning in assignments and was placed on academic probation. During this time, I worked in retail and I would do some of my coworkers' hair at their homes. My last semester in college, I resigned from my retail job and started working part-time in a hair salon. I was completely focused on doing hair, but my father's statement began to make sense to me because if things did not work out in the hair industry, I at least would have a degree I could use to obtain a job. Therefore, I encouraged myself to finish school. In 2005, I earned my degree.

After I received my degree, I began my career as a cosmetologist at a franchise hair salon in Aiken, South Carolina. The commute from Blackville, South Carolina, to Aiken was almost a one-hour drive each way. I chose to work for commission because I did not have many clients and wanted to build up my list. After commuting for a period of time, I moved to Aiken with my boyfriend. I built up my clientele by perfecting my gift and through word of mouth, and I became self-employed in 2006.

After a year of self-employment, I became a mother. My son brought love, joy, and growth into my life. My son was born during the summer, weighing close to eight pounds. My boyfriend, Kelton, was by my side for forty-two hours while I was in labor. When it was time for me to push, my father and Kelton stood by my side for two hours. It was a healthy birth and worth every second.

After a few months of maternity leave, I returned to work and began to have abdominal pain. I made an appointment with my gynecologist, who performed a cervical exam and determined that my pain was a side effect of my birth control. A year passed, and I was still experiencing abdominal pain, so I took powdered aspirin to try to relieve the pain.

One day, I was feeling constipated and noticed my stool was very narrow and filled with blood. I did not worry about it at the time and thought it was a result of being constipated, but the abdominal pain and narrow stools with blood became frequent. I Googled my symptoms, and colon cancer appeared as a result. I ignored it because the website stated that colon cancer was found in men and women at the age of fifty or older. I was twenty-seven. The pain was becoming unbearable, so I decided to go the emergency room. I did not have any medical insurance at the time, so the doctor would not examine me. He gave me a morphine shot and some special dye called "contrast" to take home with me. He told me that he would call me in the morning to see if the pain had ceased.

That night, I slept in a seated position on the sofa because the pain was unbearable. The emergency room doctor called me the next morning, and I told him I was still in pain, so he gave me the directions for the contrast. I had to drink the contrast to help highlight the areas of my body being examined during the CT scan. A few hours later, Kelton took me back to the hospital, where my mother met us. When I got there, the emergency room doctor told me what I was experiencing sounded like I could have cancer. The emergency room doctor had to convince the gastroenterologist to do further exams on me because he said I was too young to have colon cancer.

After my exam, the gastroenterologist and radiologist entered my room. The gastroenterologist's face was red, his eyes filled with water. He told me it was cancer. He said, "Due to the size of the mass, it looks like it has been there for several years." He apologized to me and said, "This is like being bit by a snake." In his experience, it was very rare for a twenty-seven-year-old to have cancer. My body went numb, and I could not respond to him. He looked in my eyes and said, "I am going to do everything in my power to help you."

The next morning, I had emergency surgery, which was my first time having major surgery. While the nurse prepared me for surgery, my parents, youngest sister, Kelton, his mother, and his grandmother were all in the waiting room. I felt nervous because the gastroenterologist told me there was a chance that the cancer could spread throughout other parts of my body once he made the incision. He said some of the cancer cells could break away from the tumor and travel to other parts of my body through the bloodstream or the lymphatic system.

When they took me into the surgery room, I felt calm after my moment of nervousness. My parents introduced me to God at a young age. I realized if I had faith the size of a mustard seed, it could move mountains. Meaning, just the small amount of belief that I would survive this was enough for me to know I would. I believed that I would live and not die, as my eyes closed slowly.

After my surgery, I recovered in the intensive care unit for the remainder of that day and then was placed in a regular hospital room. The next day, my doctor came to my room to give me and my family an update on my surgery. He said after he had made the incision, five pounds of fluid flowed out of my body. He had to remove four feet of my colon. The oncologist would let me know the stage of my cancer at a later date to determine how long I needed to take chemotherapy. I was devastated because I thought I was healed once I had recovered from surgery. I had no idea that cancer had stages.

I stayed at the hospital for one week and was discharged on Christmas Eve in 2008. I had an almost foot-long incision with staples down the middle of my stomach, causing my body to be sore for a couple of weeks. I was in so much pain and felt like I was starting to lose faith. I asked God, why me? I was young and had started a family and a career. Even though I had faith, I still questioned why this had happened and if I were going to survive. Would the cancer come back? If so, what if it spread? Did the doctors get it all out? And why did God allow this to happen to me? I knew that God allows things to happen so that we can learn to trust Him more, so I began to ask God questions during my prayer time. I sought after God more. I took more time to pray, read the Bible, and sit quietly so that I may hear God more.

A month after my surgery, Kelton took me to my follow-up appointment with my gastroenterologist, who was very honest and upfront. He was a very caring doctor who seemed to have my best interest at heart. During my consultation with the doctor, Kelton received a phone call and had to leave the room.

My doctor said, "You are too good for him."

At that point, Kelton and I had been together for almost three years, and our son was one year old. I looked at my doctor, confused because he didn't know him.

I asked him, "Why do you say that?"

He repeated, "You are too good for him."

Kelton returned to the room, and the doctor continued with my consultation. He said my scar was healing very well. He scheduled another appointment and referred me to an oncologist to have a port inserted for chemotherapy. When Kelton and I got in the car, I told him what my doctor had said about him.

He gave me a puzzled look and said, "He don't even know me!"

After my doctor's comment, I thought about our past relationship problems and wondered why he had left the room to answer a call while my doctor was discussing my fragile life and death situation. I did not take the conversation any further because I was too tired to argue, and after all, my doctor didn't know Kelton.

A few weeks later, my parents and I met with the oncologist. The oncologist told us that I had stage III colon cancer and it was in three of my surrounding lymph nodes. My heart felt like it had hit the floor. Then, he said I had to take twelve cycles of chemotherapy, which would take six months to complete. I felt like I was out of breath and about to lose my mind. I was twenty-seven years old with a one-year-old child, unemployed, and diagnosed with stage III colon cancer. I cannot remember my parents' reaction to my prognosis.

After I learned I would be going through chemotherapy, I wanted to be a beacon of hope for others going through the same trial as me. I put on a Valentine's Day Ball to raise money for a cancer society. I had outpatient surgery for my implanted port and the Valentine's Day Ball within the same week. My mother, Kelton, and I planned it. The turnout was wonderful. It was a semi-formal to formal event, and my mother and her twin sister elegantly decorated the venue in a red, black, and white color scheme. I wore a red gown with beading all over it, and Kelton wore a black suit with a red tie. We served a full-course meal, non-alcoholic and alcoholic beverages and had a photographer to take souvenir photographs. The live band played R&B music, and I was able to raise four thousand dollars. I started my journey with cancer already walking in remission.

A few weeks before I began chemotherapy, Kelton lost his job, so he took me to most of my treatments. We continued to make ends meet in spite of our circumstances because he received unemployment benefits. I also had savings because my father taught me at an early age how to save money for rainy days.

My first cycle of chemotherapy went very well, but my second cycle did not. Kelton would drop me off and pick me up at the cancer center, where I received intravenous treatments. I would not wish cancer on my worst enemy. It was painful when the nurse stuck me in my chest where the port was located. I had to sit in a recliner for four hours one day and three hours the next day. I was too weak to take care of my son after my treatments, so Kelton's mother and my youngest sister would help us out with him. The medicine would flow through my body, and within an hour, I would become weak. Every Tuesday after I had my treatment, I would vomit, and sometimes Kelton would clean it up. The treatments made me lose my appetite for a couple of days after. My strength would go up and down like a roller coaster. This caused me to become depressed and I was prescribed antidepressants. I would regain my strength one week and lose it the next. In an attempt to resolve some of my depression, after taking three months of chemotherapy, I decided to go back to work at the salon.

One day, I was sitting in the treatment room, and I received a phone call about my best friend and her mother being involved in a bad car accident. After I hung up the phone, I was in a state of shock. My friend was in surgery, and her mother had passed away. I called another friend to check on her. She avoided telling me the full truth because she did not want to upset me while I was going through chemotherapy. Every time I called to check on her, she would tell me she was "okay."

A few days after the accident, my mother called me and asked if I wanted to go to the hospital to see my best friend because the doctor did not know if she was going to survive through the night. My heart dropped. As I entered the room with my mother and cousin, I could see that my friend was badly swollen and her whole body was shaking from the power of the ventilator she was hooked up to. I wanted to touch her, but I did not have enough strength. I knew my best friend was gone. I left her room with my family and went straight to the elevator and began screaming at the top of my lungs. After I got off the elevator, my family tried to calm me down by making me sit on a bench in the hospital lobby. A strange lady walked up while they were trying to calm me down. The lady started praying over me while she held me in her arms. I became calm enough to walk to the car, tears still running down my face. I cried the whole hour it took for my mother to get back home. I stayed at my parent's house that night.

The next morning, my mother came in my room and told me my best friend had passed away, leaving three young children behind. As the tears fell down my face, all I thought about was the conversation the two of us had one day. She told me that if something were to happen to her mother, she might as well be buried with her because their bond was very tight. At that moment, I realized that it is possible to speak things into existence.

Toward the end of my treatments, I became sick and tired of being sick. I was getting ready to receive my eleventh treatment and decided that I wasn't going to do any more treatments. A cosmetologist, I always kept my hair, makeup, and nails done, but that day, I took a shower and lay around in my pajamas all day. I lied and told Kelton I didn't have to go to treatment that day. However, one of my nurses called to see why I hadn't made it to treatment. I had developed close relationships with the nurses. I cried out to her that I was tired of the treatments, sickness, and vomiting.

At this point, I felt like fighting the cancer was killing me more than the cancer itself! The inside of my hands and the bottom of my feet had turned dark. I had thrush on my tongue and tingling in my fingers and toes from the chemotherapy. The skin on my face was darker and smoother, but I never lost my hair. I barely weighed one hundred pounds.

Mentally, I was in a low state and I wanted to give up. I felt like my life was about to end because I had to deal with the death of my best friend and her mother and my chemotherapy at the same time. I didn't care if I survived or not because at least I would be with my best friend and her mother.

The nurse begged me not to give up. She told me, "Candace, you have to praise your way through it." Meaning, I needed to celebrate and thank God in advance for my healing. She ultimately agreed that I should take the day off and come back the next day after I had gotten a break and much needed rest.

The day that I had this breakdown, Kelton was gone all day and my son was with Kelton's mother. I didn't even have the strength to argue with him about being gone all day when he came home because I was actually glad he had been away from me. He could tell that I wasn't myself and asked what was wrong. I told him, "I'm sick and tired of everything, including you!"

I was wondering at this point if the doctor's statement that day was starting to make sense. Though Kelton was there for me during this ordeal, our relationship continued to have many ups and downs. He continued bad habits and hanging out in the streets from time to time. I wasn't prepared to break up with him though. I was in the midst of fighting cancer. I was vulnerable and I truly loved and believed in our relationship.

The next day, I went to my treatment. I was determined to live for the sake of my son and my family. All I did was think of my son and how his life would be without me and how my family would feel. I was taught to pray and ask God for what I want Him to do in my life, and if it is in His will, it will be done. I had to cry out to God for help because I believed He could help me get through everything! I told God if He gave me another chance to live, I would promise to live my life to the fullest. I stopped stressing over my illness, and I released it to Him for my miracle, blessing, and breakthrough.

When I came home after treatment, Kelton had already cooked dinner. He asked me if I was hungry or if I wanted something to drink. I told him I didn't have an appetite, so he fixed me something to drink. He was acting really nice that day. We sat on the sofa and watched television. I began to get tired, and he got up to run my bath water for me.

He came back and sat on the sofa and said, "I finished running your water for you."

"Thank you," I replied.

"You don't have much longer to go and it will be over."

During the summer of 2009, I finished my chemotherapy. A few weeks after, I took a CT scan to determine if there were any signs of cancer. The oncologist said the results from the CT scan did not show any signs of cancer. He told me to call the gastroenterologist to have a colonoscopy done in six months. I had to see the oncologist every month for blood work until it was time for my colonoscopy. Within the six months waiting period, Kelton and I were at a happier place in our relationship and we became engaged.

My mother and I met with the gastroenterologist a few days before he did my colonoscopy. While we were sitting in the exam room, he noticed my engagement ring and sarcastically said to me, "So you are going to marry the guy?"

I sarcastically replied back, "Yes," and we all laughed it off because I had already told my mother what he had said the last time.

A few days later, I had my colonoscopy, and the result showed no sign of cancer! (Now, I see the oncologist twice a year and will continue for the rest of my life to have blood work done as a precaution against cancer.)

Once my cancer was in remission, I felt excited about my future. After I defeated cancer, some people around my age started asking me about my symptoms because they were having problems with their stomachs. I was happy to share and educate other young people about ways to take precautions in health and how to develop a relationship with their doctors to ensure they could catch the signs early.

I had to rebuild most of my clientele that I had in Aiken because I relocated back home to Blackville after I finished chemotherapy. It did not take long for me to rebuild my clientele because my work became quite popular from sharing pictures on social media, and the quality of my work established a strong brand for me. God has blessed me with a very loving and supportive salon owner and a clientele full of loyal, strong, and beautiful women, each of whom I love wholeheartedly.

In the years after my final treatment, I spent most of my time behind a salon chair, listening to music, enhancing my clients' beauty, motivating them to get through their life challenges, and showing them how much I appreciated them. At times, some of my clients motivated me as well. Every day I am at work, I have several of my clients tell me how much better I made them look and feel before they left. My clients are like my second family. We have laughed, cried, and grown together. My purpose as a cosmetologist and cancer survivor is to touch more hearts than hair.

## #LessonLearned

Each survivor reacts differently to his or her diagnosis. Some survivors will need help during and after cancer treatments. Some survivors will keep their journey through cancer a secret because of emotional numbness and other feelings. Some survivors will have the urge to tell their journey to others, hoping that their experience with cancer will help save someone else's life. Some survivors will experience relationship difficulties, and others will develop stronger relationships. Life is too short. Your age has nothing to do with being diagnosed with cancer nor facing death. Questioning God is okay; learning to sit and be quiet allows you to gain clarity over the challenges of your life. I learned that sometimes God will show you favor because of someone else's faith.

## #WorthTheCost

I survived it! The condition that you are in is not your conclusion. You can turn your pain into purpose. Whenever God has a destiny for you, death has to back off! God placed grace and mercy on my life to still be here for my son. I feel like cancer made me more mature. I'm stronger and wiser both spiritually and mentally. I fear God. I value my life and my family more. Having a happy and healthy life is important to me now. My family and friends were very supportive and amazing during my storm. Now that I am in remission, I have the strength to beat the odds in life.

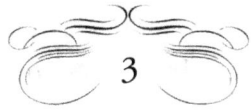

# My Marriage Behind a Closed Door

Marriage can be a beautiful thing if the two people within the relationship work hard for it. It does not come with a lifetime warranty, so be mindful how you take care of it. Marriage doesn't fix people; it reveals the rawness of the two people in it. Marriage isn't about perfection but about loving a person despite their imperfections and seeing how your lives are able to create something beautiful. Marriage will make you do things you never thought you would do to protect it.

The man I fell in love with was a few years older than me and did not have a perfect past. We attended high school together, and I had a secret crush on him, but I did not tell him this until we were in a relationship. During the start of our relationship, he was on probation, unemployed with a suspended driver's license, and a frequent alcohol drinker. I believed my husband had more potential within him than things to offer me. I surrounded him with love and motivation while helping him financially to become a better person.

Once Kelton and I started dating, some of the people who knew him would tell me how much of a positive change they noticed in him. He had a very funny and caring personality. He would always have a joke to tell, and he showed simple acts of kindness by ironing my clothes for work and fixing my plate of food for dinner. He always told me how much he loved me. As a father, Kelton stood by my side when I was giving birth to our son and fighting cancer. He was a good father and also a father figure to my nephew. To provide, he worked as an environmental maintenance worker for a subcontractor at a nuclear plant. He was a handyman who loved to cook, and that turned me on even more because I didn't have to cook all of the time, nor bother my father about fixing things for me. Kelton was the man I wanted to spend the rest of my life with. I was in love with him, he was willing to help when I needed a favor, we learned from each other, and he would compliment me.

Despite all the wonderful things about Kelton, we dated for five years with some stumbling blocks. It was difficult at times for us to stay on the same page. During this part of our relationship, I felt irritated and lonely. He would hang out with his friends well into the night. I would hear things about his disloyalty and I would break up with him not only because of what I heard but the actions he showed. He would always make a promise to change if I gave him another chance. We managed to get through all of our issues because of our love and my willingness to be forgiving.

In 2010, at his parents' house, Kelton handed me an envelope and said, "Someone sent you some mail."

The stamped envelope had my name on it with his parents' address, and the return address was our son's school's address. I was puzzled because I knew I didn't use his parents' address on any paperwork at our son's school. I opened the envelope and pulled out the folded piece of paper. On the paper were individual colorful stickers that spelled out, "Will you marry me?" Kelton got down on one knee, with a ring in his hand, and asked me to marry him.

In 2011, at the age of thirty, I became his wife. Our wedding day was everything I dreamed it would be. Our wedding colors were pool blue and canary yellow. I arrived at New Life Baptist Church in a black limousine Hummer. My father was waiting for me at the church door. I grabbed ahold of my father's left arm while we waited for the moment he would walk me down the aisle. The doors opened, and my whole wedding party was in formation. My ten bridesmaids were standing at the front of the church in elegant dresses, holding bouquets of fresh roses, hydrangeas, and tulips and the lighted candle in memory of my best friend was on a tall single candelabra behind them. The ten groomsmen wore black tuxedos, tulips pinned to their lapels. As I took my first step on my custom hand-painted aisle runner, I looked in Kelton's eyes with a serious look that said, "this is the moment we have been waiting for." Kelton was wearing a black tuxedo. I could see love and adoration in his eyes when he saw me walk into the church.

My wedding ceremony was beautiful and filled with love. The audience was full of family and friends and classmates. Standing at the altar with Kelton felt like a new beginning of life and a happily ever after. During marriage counseling, we both understood that we were not only making marriage vows to each other but to God. I stood at the altar and took every word of my marriage vows seriously. The things that Kelton did before we got married were no longer an issue to me. In my heart, I felt like we were going to grow old together. I left everything that happened in our past behind us as we walked away from the altar.

Our reception venue was a beautiful scene, filled with fresh flower arrangements and china on every table. A chocolate fountain surrounded with fruits was in the back, not far from our five-tier cake. Everyone danced, and for months afterward, our guests talked about how much they enjoyed themselves and how beautiful our wedding was.

Being married felt lovely. On our days off from work, we would go places together. We ensured we had family time. We supported each other's goals and provided for our household as a team. We were very affectionate and appreciative of one another. Kelton would gladly call me his wife. All I would hear him say was my wife, my wife, my wife! Despite our challenges in our relationship prior to getting married, we decided to make our lives work together. Our first year as husband and wife were great. I thought we had truly overcome all the challenges. I thought marriage had fixed us.

After a year and a half of being married, things started to change. My husband returned to spending most of his time running the streets. He would come in the house late as if he were still single. He spent more time enjoying his relationships with his friends than building one with me. I felt he would rather spend time around a barbecue grill with his friends instead of with his family. When one of his friends would call for him to do something, he would not waste time to help, but when I would ask him to do something, he would take his time. I felt he was getting too comfortable with making choices I felt were bad for our marriage. I got tired of telling him, "Keep running with your friends and watch how fast you will not have a wife!"

I could not get him to understand that some of his friends wanted to see him do well but not better than them. If you hang out with five ideal people who don't value marriage or family, you will be the sixth person sooner or later. He stopped valuing our marriage and family, and he completely stopped being a provider after he had a pay cut in his job. He used his paycheck to only pay his personal bills. As a wife, I had my husband's back when he fell short. I started providing for our home without his assistance because he did not have enough money leftover from his paycheck to cover any of our household bills. I also did not want him to walk around without any money in his pockets.

As a result of our problems, we argued more than we made love. I tried to explain to him that I understood that he took a pay cut and could not help provide the way he used to, but what I could not understand was the way he would have enough money to go to a nightclub but not enough for our household bills. The husband's job is to protect and provide for his family. I was raised to believe that if you are a husband and you have two dollars of your paycheck leftover, those two dollars belong to your household ahead of your form of solo entertainment.

Kelton went from being a good husband all of the time to being a good husband only when he wanted me to forgive him. I was constantly forgiving him for the same thing. I was working harder on my marriage than I was on my job! I knew something was wrong, but I could not put my hands on it, and I did not want to end our marriage based off of assumptions, so I prayed and asked God to reveal it to me and I left it alone.

After being married a little over two years, my heart was shattered into pieces. My husband's body language and my intuition led me to find out I was betrayed. In 2013, on a Friday afternoon, I suggested adding Kelton's motorcycle to the auto insurance policy we had together because he could save more money, and he agreed. The agent needed an electronic signature. I went to check my email for the documents the agent sent me, but Kelton had not logged out of his email account. I did exactly what you are probably thinking. I searched through his entire email account and found some of his old direct messages from his social media account that had been sent to his email. I saw one message he sent to a woman two months after we had gotten married, telling her he was thinking about her! I called the agent and told him to disregard adding the motorcycle.

Kelton came home later that evening and asked me if I had added the motorcycle. I told him yes. I got his laptop and told him to take a look at what the agent sent. He looked at the screen and immediately panicked because on the screen were the direct messages from his social media account. I was pissed! He tried to explain with lies. He slept in the guest room in our house for a week. I know the streets missed him that week because he did not go anywhere but to work and back home.

I was tired of communicating only to hear his lies. During that week, I watched his body language. Believe it or not, body language has a voice of its own. My husband started looking at me with a sad expression. He would walk around the house with his hands in his pocket, his head held down. He moved like he wanted to tell me something but did not know how. Sometimes, he would just sit and rub his hand across his forehead.

Exactly one week after I exposed my husband's direct messages to him, he drank some liquor, fell into a deep sleep on the sofa, and left his cell phone on the kitchen island. He had never left his phone unattended. You would have thought it was his third hand. Because of seeing his inappropriate messages from the week before, I took the memory card out of his phone. The next day, when he was looking for it, I pretended as if I did not know what had happened to it. Later that day when he left the house, I put his memory card into his laptop. I printed all of his current and deleted text messages from his card. I needed to know what else he was hiding. I thought we had left behind the challenges of our relationship at the altar. I had learned that falling in love with someone's potential to change will only give you their reality.

When Kelton returned home, some of my family were visiting. I tried to wait for them to leave so I could confront him, but I was still pissed from the week before, and my anger took over my soul. I came out of the bedroom to approach him, and when I entered the living room, he was sitting in a chair talking to my family. I stood in front of him with the stack of printed text messages.

I asked him, "Who did you text, 'don't get my dick hard?'"

He pretended to act dumb as if he did not know what I was talking about, so I acted dumb with my fist. I beat his ass! I started punching him in his face with my fist, he stood up, and I grabbed his neck with my hands while choking him. He tried to run away, and I grabbed his shirt, ripping it halfway off. While I was beating his ass, all I thought about was how much I sacrificed to try to make him into what I believed would be a better person. Some of my family members had to pull me off of him. I saw blood on me and thought I was bleeding, but it was his blood! Kelton was too scared to do anything. I showed out so bad, all of my visiting family members thought they were about to witness a murder!

Everybody left the inside of my house and stood in the yard, except me. My mother was at a funeral, and a family member called and texted her to come home immediately. Kelton took his laptop outside and set it—his evidence of betrayal—on fire. When my mother walked in my room, I was packing Kelton's clothes in trash bags. I was so angry and did not hear one word she said. I took the trash bags filled with his clothes and threw them out of my bedroom window. I told him he was leaving just like he came and to get the fuck out of my yard. I also told him to text all of his whores to tell them he was homeless! But already, I had contacted a few of them myself and told them for him.

After Kelton left, I waited for the laptop to cool down before I retrieved it from the burn barrel. Everything was burned except the hard drive, so I removed it from his laptop. That was the only time in my life I used my college degree—to retrieve information from his hard drive. I do not know which feeling was worse: finding out about more instances where I was betrayed or finding out it had happened with some of the women who were at our wedding. If I could have gotten away with murder, I would have killed him!

I was hurt, angry, bitter, and embarrassed. My doctor had tried to tell me I was too good for Kelton; he'd known just by watching Kelton leave the room to answer a phone call. The thought crossed my mind that I should have listened to the person who saved my life! I tried hard to justify his betrayal, but I could not. I was a loyal wife. I provided financially when he was laid off from his job and after his pay cut. I was always supportive and helped him when nobody else could. I went above and beyond for this man. I could not understand what I had done to deserve what he did to me and neither could he. I realized trying to make my husband happy was making me hurt myself, so instead of me waiting on his heart to change, I changed mine instead. I never imagined filing for a divorce.

One morning while I was in the shower, I had to ask God to give me a sign that I made the right decision filing for a divorce. When I opened my bedroom door, I noticed my bed was made up. My five-year-old son had made up my queen-size bed for the first time in his life. At that moment, I knew my son and I were going to be all right. Kelton was served divorce papers less than three weeks after he left. He was no longer the man I fell in love with; he was the man who betrayed me.

I learned that marriage does not always mean forever. I had this vision in my mind that my husband would stay committed to our vows and that we would build an empire together. What I know is that as a giver, I hadn't paid much attention to the warning signs and how I was making myself vulnerable by always forgiving him for his same bad choices. I learned I couldn't expect my husband to appreciate a home that was given to him without investment in it because that was his own choice. Most importantly, I realized that when you pray and ask God to reveal something, He will do it.

The divorce process was stressful. Kelton and I still had to communicate because of our child. Sometimes, whenever he brought our son back home, we would talk. Kelton was not remorseful; he told someone that I would take him back in six months. Instead of owning up to the truth, he tried to buy me material things to act as a bandage for my wounds.

One night, I heard someone knocking so hard on the back door of my house, so I got out of my bed to answer the door. It was Kelton, and he was drunk. He tried to hurt me by telling me he had a girlfriend with a nice house and a good job and he wanted to have a child with her. He failed to mention anything about her character. He was hoping I would change my mind because he thought I feared he would have a better life with someone else.

Despite what transpired, I never felt threatened by a mistress or the next woman because of my self-confidence. Kelton's actions gave me more confirmation that I made the right decision to file for a divorce. His attempts to make me jealous or envious of his new relationship by trying to replace everything he had lost with me with her were fruitless. My love could never be bought. There was no need for me to feel like I was being replaced by another woman but instead *released* from this relationship. With me, Kelton had a nice house with a good wife who had a good job and a child, and I believed he still didn't see value in that. I slammed the door in his face. Yet despite knowing that divorcing him was the right thing to do, I felt devastated. Deep down, I had wanted my marriage to work. I realized Kelton was in my life to teach me some of my biggest lessons and to give me one of my biggest blessings—my son.

Kelton found other ways to keep himself in my life on a constant basis. I was raised in a very valuable, spiritual, and family-oriented family. My father and some of my other family members had a close relationship with my soon-to-be ex-husband. When people want to hurt you, they sometimes try to use the people closest to you to do so. They try to manipulate you by using people close to you. Kelton did this by developing a relationship with my father.

When Kelton realized I was serious about the divorce and nothing he said or did was going to make me change my mind, he used my father to get a reaction from me. He invited him to his cookouts and other events, and they rode their motorcycles together. I began to feel betrayed by my father because I could not understand how he could smile and socialize with him after he hurt me. It was hard for me to allow my wounds to heal because Kelton was always around. When you are trying to heal, you have to remove yourself from the source of the pain. In this case, it was Kelton, but his relationship with my family made it difficult for me. One day, I cried my heart out to my father and tried to explain to him that the only reason Kelton invited him to things was to upset me and to make himself look innocent. My father defended his relationship with him. It hurt me so bad, I stopped talking to my father for a month.

Can you imagine being hurt at the same time by the man you married and the man who helped bring you into this world? How would you feel if you were betrayed by your spouse only to see your closest family members remain close to them? Can you imagine thinking that the wounds of betrayal were healed, but once married, you discover that the marriage you thought erased the past only revealed the same issues? How can you regain your strength as a woman after being betrayed repeatedly?

---

### #LessonLearned

**Evaluate your partner. Your relationship is meant to build one another up, not drag each other down. If you and your (future) spouse have different values, this can have a great impact on decision-making, raising your children, and determining the importance of faith in their life. You may have the faith that your partner will change, but there is no way you can control their faith. So, if before marriage, you have problems with trust and with your significant other's hanging out, alcohol drinking, and financial abilities, be prepared for the chance of that happening in your marriage.**

## #WorthTheCost

Waiting for someone with whom you share the same heritage and spiritual values can be rewarding. I believed in my husband and loved him through his faults because I believed that God was going to transform his values. But not everyone wants to change. I felt used and exhausted, and my marriage wasn't growing, so I used my intuition to know when to stay or leave. Some people are only looking for stability in others. I believe a common ground marriage is a happily ever after because it will be a safe place for each person to grow and learn without judgment. I believe the husband should be the head of the household and the wife is the multiplier. I was taught if you give me a house, I'll make it a home. If you give me a seed, I'll make you a family. If you buy me groceries, I'll cook you a meal. If you give me money, I'll make an investment. If you show me admiration, I'll show you love. If you give me foolishness, I'll find my peace.

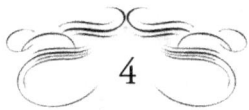

# Don't Take Your Marriage for Granted

Some people don't view marriage the same, or they take the purpose of a marriage for granted. Many think that when you join in union with another person, you can continue on living your life as you did before you took your vows, not realizing that when you marry, you join as one with another person. I have come to know that praying and ensuring you are equally yoked with your partner before getting married is important.

In the Bible and as I grew up, I learned that when you marry, you are supposed to love your spouse as Christ loved the church, which means you pour yourself into your marriage. Your spouse's happiness becomes important to you, and their priorities become your priorities. You give them compliments, ensure they feel appreciated, and strive to be honest and forthcoming so that you build trust. I have come to know that marriage helps the two individuals in it become better together. You are strong without them, but together, you are stronger and more powerful.

If a person feels like they can have the same habits from their single life in their married life, marriage may not be for you, and if you decide to marry, ultimately your single lifestyle will treat you like the weather: when it is a beautiful day, everyone is around; but when it rains, no one wants to stay around. I don't think anyone gets into a relationship wanting to feel like they aren't important or a priority to their mate, but can you imagine how you would feel if you took your spouse for granted?

I believe that when people cheat and are unfaithful in their marriage, it is a sign of inner weakness and an inability to express feelings of unhappiness. Sometimes, people in a relationship aren't sure if they should leave the relationship or not, so they become unfaithful. However, I believe that if you are willing to cheat, then you should be strong enough to leave the relationship. You may think someone loves you, but when their love is tested, they can prove you wrong.

Another issue in relationships is when people use random people as a sounding board to problems in their household. Having a trusted confidant is good, but people in the streets should never be privy to what your married life is like. The problems you are having in your marriage will not be fixed in the streets. When something goes wrong, those same people have no loyalty to your marriage or reason to make it a priority.

The people in the streets will not drive any distance to be in your presence when things go wrong. The people in the streets will not kneel down beside you and pray for you when things go wrong. The people in the streets will not be there until the end when things go wrong.

It's important to value your close relationships like your marriage, children, and family. Most importantly, make sure God is in your marriage and your circle of friends because when something goes wrong and as time goes on, the more the people will disappear.

I had to learn these lessons the hard way during my marriage and relationship with Kelton. I didn't realize the magnitude of the decision we made to marry and how unprepared we were. While I felt I did everything within my power to protect and cover my marriage, I didn't feel he valued it in the same way. Because of that, my belief that marriage would change him or make us better was completely wrong. However, I learned a great deal about friendship and myself. I learned that I needed to change my views and some of my ways. I needed to get better.

## #LessonLearned

Marriage can be as beautiful as the two people make it, based on their decisions. It doesn't mean there will be no challenges, but the challenges come to reveal an opportunity for the two people to hopefully get better. Deciding to get married shouldn't be a decision you take lightly. Invest in those who invest in themselves first.

## #WorthTheCost

Your blessing is in what is left, not lost.

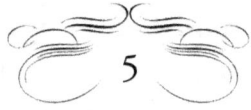

## Make Me Over

Brokenness in your life can turn you into a person you weren't created to be. The cracks are an entrance for spirits to enter your mind and heart. The spirit of anger, bitterness, and unforgiveness influenced me to stoop down to a person's level when they were behaving poorly. I've learned that you have to teach people how to treat and respect you. I had to go through seventeen months of torture before my divorce was finalized, but I refused to live the rest of my life being tortured and I refused to live the rest of my life with an angry, bitter, and unforgiving heart.

All of the things that I did in reaction to my soon-to-be ex-husband's behavior were getting out of hand. I began to notice the lies Kelton would tell on me and about our relationship. Once I finally accepted the truth about who he had always been, I began to see the lies clearly. I had ignored many of the signs because I wanted to love him and

I thought by loving him I would change him. In reality, it was me who changed. I realized my own issues and had to confront how I gave. The more he lied on me, the more I told the truth about him and the more I saw things within myself I needed to change. I was living my life like a scorned woman—because I was.

During our divorce process, I continued to behave poorly and react to Kelton's actions. He lied and told people I had betrayed him. I offered him copies of my cell phone call records in return for all of his, but he wouldn't agree. After he told that lie, I posted evidence of his betrayal on social media. I posted pictures of the stack of printed text messages and the burnt laptop. He went around telling people that I was crazy—I wasn't crazy but smarter than a mistress. Kelton told someone that I was not affectionate, and that person came back and told me what he said. I told them that Kelton forgot to tell them that he was not paying any bills in the house and "...tired pussy does not get wet!"

Every time I saw Kelton, I would get angry all over again. I was reacting to everything Kelton did as my own way to get revenge. Even though deep down I knew it would not make things any better, I didn't know any other way to express my anger and hurt. I did what I knew how to do. Eventually, I realized my own madness.

One day, I spoke with my attorney on the phone and I became angry after she told me what Kelton was asking for.

After I hung up with her, I called him and told him he was leaving our marriage the same way he came! He came in the marriage with nothing and he was leaving with nothing. He hung up while I was still talking. I got in my car and went around to his parents' house. I saw his vehicle in the yard. I got out of my car and knocked on the door. He came to the door and noticing it was me, wouldn't open it. I went around to his bedroom window and started knocking on the window. I was mad as hell, and before I knew it, I had knocked his bedroom window out with my fist, cutting my right hand. I felt like I was about to go to jail, so I got back in my car and left. Later on, that evening, I called Kelton's father to apologize and offered to replace the window, but his father accepted my apology and told me not to worry about it.

I was out of control in my mind with anger. I had to realize that my marriage wasn't what I wanted it to be and that somehow, I had failed. My soon-to-be ex's betrayal revealed more than just his issues; it revealed my own. Having an angry, bitter, and unforgiving heart was allowing me to hurt myself and others.

---

In 2014, my divorce was finalized. The day of court, before our final hearing, Kelton walked up to my car and tapped on my window. I could not believe he walked around seventeen months during the divorce process doing whatever he wanted to do believing that I would not divorce him. I nicely looked at him through my car window and said, "I will see you in court!"

As we were leaving the courthouse, Kelton sarcastically asked me if he could take me out for lunch. I ignored him. As much as I tried not to, I still continued to react poorly to his behavior. Every time I reacted to Kelton, he would say, "You are doing this because you still love me." I loved him, but I was not in love with him anymore, and he could not see that. Whenever I tried to be nice to my ex-husband, he took my kindness as weakness and believed we were getting back together. After the divorce was finalized, Kelton still came around to my parents' house several times a week. Sometimes, my son would be with Kelton's parents while Kelton spent time with my father. My parents' and I are neighbors. I felt like I wasn't even divorced from him.

Eventually, Kelton did exactly what he told me he was going to do. He started a relationship with one of his mistresses. Her name was Justine. She worked for the military and lived states away. She was raised in a town close to where Kelton and I lived while we were married. She became pregnant by him four months after our divorce was finalized. He tried hard to keep their child a secret, but someone mentioned it to me. When I mentioned it to him, he said, "I see you did all of your homework!"

I did not believe he cared about our son's feelings. I believed my son was old enough to understand what was happening with his family and that his father had decided to start a new relationship and have another child. I was very concerned about my son and his relationship with his father. My son was eight years old during the divorce and was a very bright child. I continued to keep things as normal as I could even in all the madness. My son played football on the weekends and loved it. His father would practice with him and attend all of his games. They had a really great bond.

My son loved and looked up to his father. However, midway through the divorce, Kelton's behavior changed. He wasn't spending as much time with our son as he used to. It bothered our son a little but not much because Kelton's father was also a father figure to our son and my nephew, and he would spend a lot of time with the both of them.

One day, Kelton dropped our son off at my house. My family and friends were standing in my yard when he arrived. Kelton thought he was going to stand in my yard while he talked to my family and friends. I told him to get out of my yard. Then we started arguing. I ripped the paper tag off of his new vehicle and kicked it. I would have put a dent in it, but I was wearing sandals. My son was there to witness this scene. He began to cry so hard that it was like someone was killing him. I realized that I was taking this situation too far and hurting my child in the meantime. My anger toward my ex-husband wasn't worth my child's hurt. As a mother, I needed to reevaluate how I was behaving.

A few months after I kicked Kelton's vehicle, someone accidently hit my parked, brand-new car with their car and left the scene. From that moment on, I knew I had to find my place of peace and remove myself from trying to control the situation because I was not only hurting myself but my son. I was acting like I didn't have anything to lose in life, and I was being a bad example to my son.

One day, I asked my son about his visit with his father and he began to cry because he feared he was going to start an argument. I asked him if he was around Justine and he said yes. I asked him if Justine treated him nicely. He said yes. I told my son it was all right for him to be around Justine but to let me know if she mistreated him. Deep down, I didn't want him to be around her. I didn't know anything about her character and I never saw her in person. However, I viewed her as a demoralized woman without family values because of her willingness to be in a relationship with my ex while we were still married. When it came to my son, however, I realized I had to make some sacrifices within myself so he could be happy. The worst pain I think a child can ever experience is the absence of a parent. I prayed and asked God to protect my son while he was away from me.

After I told my son it was all right for him to be around Justine, he would come home and tell me how she would buy him things. I wondered if buying him things was the only way she connected with him. I realized that some children can be brainwashed easily. I told my son not to feel like he had to like her because she brought him things but to always tell her thank you. I really didn't like her buying him things because I felt like she was only doing it as long as her relationship with Kelton was strong. I believed Kelton would end up cheating and lying to her like he did to me, which would end her relationship with my child.

Once Justine had her child, a girl, my son and I would go shopping and he would buy his sister gifts. He had her picture as his wallpaper on his cell phone. After seeing how much my son cared about his sister, I started feeling like I wanted to build a relationship with her.

I refused to continue arguing about Kelton's opinions and lies about me, especially when it did not affect my way of living. I was making myself sick from all of the stress. I wasn't focusing on my career. I tried to heal my pain with retail therapy and alcoholic beverages, but it only helped temporarily. Sometimes, I would be in my bedroom for hours listening to gospel and R&B music, crying my heart out. I repeatedly listened to "Shifting the Atmosphere" and "Nothing Without You" by Jason Nelson. I would also play music while I took my shower. My son would be in his room watching television, playing his video game system, or playing with my nephew. I lived my life like an old piece of wood covered with metallic paint. I was beautiful on the outside but a mess on the inside.

I decided to let go of anyone and anything that was weighing me down. I had to pray for serenity and find my place of peace. I realized that you can't heal what you can't speak. I needed to talk about what I was feeling in order for me to begin healing. I would talk to some of my family, friends, and clients. Even though they would give me good advice, I never felt as though they truly understood my pain.

I had to separate, isolate, and focus on myself. I had to stop letting my trials and tribulations keep me from achieving greatness by losing my focus. I had to stop talking so much because it was giving negative people the opportunity to breathe negativity on my vision. I had to forgive myself.

I took ownership of my pain. I accepted that I was betrayed by my ex-husband and I stopped letting my ex-husband's betrayal define who I was. It was like a curse over me that I was allowing to carry into my entire life. A curse will prevent you from living your life with happiness if you allow it. I was betrayed, but I wasn't going to let it stop me from loving again because I know that I am worthy! Do you know that you are worthy?

To change my mindset, I watched inspirational videos on YouTube and attended church periodically. Whatever you do in your life, make sure you, your family, and your friends have a relationship with God because when negative things happen in your life, you need to understand that you have the power and ability to keep them from harming you. In the Bible, the scripture goes, "No weapon that is formed against thee shall prosper" (Isaiah 54:17). You don't have to be perfect to be in a relationship with God.

Over time, and as my relationship with God grew stronger, I switched the energy that I was putting into distractions and refocused it on building a closer relationship with God, allowing Him to speak to my heart. I didn't focus on earthly relationships. I didn't try to fill a void because of loneliness. When God told me to "let vengeance be His," I let it. I took that to mean that I didn't need to be angry or vengeful. I needed to focus on my own healing and do what was right for me. When God told me the battle wasn't mine, I let Him fight. God will sometimes allow you to suffer more than you can bear, but that is okay because His grace is sufficient! God will break us so that He can remake us.

When I started to feel lonely, I knew that God was always there. I refused to settle. On social media, I started to post things that I struggled with in my life, for motivational purposes only, instead of negative things. I would post pictures of hairstyles that I created on my clients. It felt like I was encouraging myself and someone else at the same time. I did this for a while, and then a few of my social media friends told me how much they were inspired by me. I had a cosmetology student direct message me to tell me that I was her idol. I came to understand that the more positive things I posted, the more I healed.

Brokenness won't give you happiness. A broken person has to be willing to fix themselves. If you try to fix a broken person while you're in a relationship with them, there is a chance that you will not be the one to enjoy the happily ever after because as soon as you think you fixed them, that's when you will realize you've lost yourself. If you ever find yourself at a broken place in your life, take your time and heal first because you can cause more hurt to yourself and someone else. You may feel like you don't have the strength to get through whatever you're going through. You may feel like you're not rising above your problems. You may feel like you're running and walking through life and getting tired. Wait on God and believe that He will renew your strength. Faith without work is dead.

I said this Bible verse to myself to keep moving forward in life:

> *"But they that wait upon the LORD shall renew their strength; they shall mount up with wings as eagles; they shall run, and not be weary; and they shall walk, and not faint."*
> Isaiah 40:31

### #LessonLearned

Children absorb a lot of what we, their parents, go through--whether we know it or not. What if your past was to resurface in your child through their behavior or life decisions? Do you know how you would handle it? Until you experience it, you may not know, but certainly as a mother, I had to learn to ask myself those exact questions as I evaluated my actions and their impact on my child. Life is a process of reaping and sowing. I wasn't being the best example to my child that I knew I could be. My peace was out of alignment.

### #WorthTheCost

Know your worth. Knowing and believing that you are worthy is a blessing. That means no one will ever have control of who you are. There will be no insecurities in your life you can't overcome. When you know your worth, you don't need the approval of others. When you know your worth, it is not your job to make others feel comfortable while they are around you. Some people will try to make you feel like you are arrogant or conceited when you know your worth. It is not your job to care about what people think of you. Continue being worthy! The moment you start feeling worthless is the moment your life will start fading away.

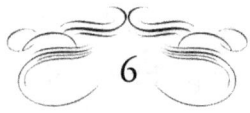

# 6

# Forgiving to Have Peace

Playing the victim in a situation is not going to fix its circumstances or change the outcome because the truth will stand regardless. For your own sanity, I believe it is necessary to apologize when you are wrong and forgive, whether you received an apology or not. If you knew the consequences behind a negative choice that you make, will you still make that choice? If they continuously forgive someone for their same negative choices, without consequences, you will not learn the lesson, and the mistreatment may continue. I have learned that when people learn how to treat you, they will continue the same behavior as long as they can predict your reaction. When you learn to set boundaries for yourself and live your life on your terms, you will minimize how other people's behaviors will impact you.

Forgiving was the hardest thing for me to do after I was betrayed. Kelton would not own up to anything he did wrong. One day, when Kelton brought our son back home, he asked to talk to me. He kept repeating, "I messed up." I told him I already knew that he messed up. I wanted to know how and why he messed up. He said the text messages were a form of entertainment, which I believed. He was enjoying the attention he was getting from these women. His unwillingness to make positive choices in our relationship, let alone respect our relationship, became clear to me.

The women were looking for a win off of the fascinating games he was running with a penis and a wallet full of lies. I felt like his decisions were more about protecting the other women and not me! I just wanted him to take accountability for his actions, and he would not. He never stopped coming around me and my family, so in order for me to make myself feel comfortable with him coming around, I had to forgive him despite his lack of remorse. I felt like Kelton was disrespecting my personal space and trying to block another man from coming into my life. I needed him to respect my life without him, like I was respecting his by spending less time with his family. I just wanted him to go and live his life with his new family and leave mine alone. Despite my frustrations, I learned that forgiveness is what we are commanded to do, but trust must be earned. Forgiveness is based on grace, and trust is built upon work.

I cannot change the bond between my father and Kelton because it was created before Kelton betrayed me. I cannot change the pain I felt from being betrayed. I cannot change what happened in my past, but forgiveness and an answered prayer for serenity allow me to accept the things I cannot change. Once I forgave Kelton, I no longer became angry when he came around me and my family.

---

#### #LessonLearned

We are all human. We have done and said things that were wrong and for which we needed forgiveness. Being overwhelmed with how others have wronged you will only fill your heart with anger. Then you will find yourself focused on hate. God's love and forgiveness are seen in our ability to love and forgive. Try living the way God would want us to live so you will not block your blessings in life.

---

#### #WorthTheCost

I know from experience that it can be a struggle when it comes to forgiveness. Even though your season may be challenging right now, it is working for your good, and when it is all over, you are going to walk away from it with more than you ever had. Your purpose is being worked out. Every storm that happens in your life does not always come from the enemy. Endure whatever is complicated so you can see what you can do, what you can take, and who you can become. At the end of your storms, you will realize your harvest was connected to every tear that ran down your face. The good who have suffered for the sake of God will win! Love, forgive, and leave revenge for God. And watch the switch-up, because the last shall be first, and the first shall be last.

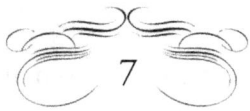

# Be Mindful of What You Do

What if the person you betrayed ultimately becomes the person you will need the most in your time of need? Imagine where your life would be if the person you need the most in your time of need had not forgiven you for betraying them.

One Sunday morning in 2016, I received a phone call from one of Kelton's family members about him being in a very bad accident. He had hit a deer while he was riding his motorcycle and had suffered a severe traumatic brain injury with a diffuse axonal injury. The doctor did not know if he was going to make it. I hung up the phone and got dressed to go to the hospital. On my way to the hospital, I prayed for healing, deliverance, and restoration over his body.

I arrived to the hospital with my parents. I looked through the window of the waiting room, where I saw Justine and Kelton's parents. I walked into the waiting room and hugged his parents. As I was walking out of the waiting room, I looked at Justine. This was my first time seeing her in person. Even though I knew she was in my son's life and thought I had made peace with her and Kelton's relationship, my emotions took over me. I almost whipped Justine's ass when I saw her. I had my hands up, ready to fight, but I caught myself after my mother told me to stop.

When I entered Kelton's room in the intensive care unit, I stood by his bedside and watched him fight for his life on a ventilator. All I could do was pray for grace and mercy. I stayed in his room for about fifteen minutes. I had just seen him a few days before his accident at my family's Thanksgiving dinner. After seeing how he looked, I became remorseful about what I did to Justine. I left his room and went to look for her.

She was standing in the hall, talking to Kelton's friend. I walked up to her and asked her if I could talk to her. While we walked down the hallway, she asked me if I was going to fight her. I told her no and apologized for what I had done to her in the waiting room. I expressed that my reaction to her was out of anger toward Kelton and his betrayal of our marriage. She accepted my apology, and we went our separate ways.

I've always had strong views about marriage and infidelity and believed that a woman in Justine's position is broken and doesn't believe in her value and worth. Though I confronted her and apologized for my behavior, I wondered why she believed it was appropriate to engage in a relationship with my husband at the time. I wondered if she thought her life would somehow be better than mine, or if she believed Kelton's lies. Though I thought about all of this and got angry and wanted to attack her, none of it meant anything anymore, as we both were facing losing Kelton—the father of our children.

A few days later, while I was visiting Kelton, I was introduced to the young lady who found him and reported the accident. Her name was Angel, and she was twenty-one years old. After I was introduced to Angel, she started telling me about the accident. Angel told me the road she found him on was the road she took to visit her friend. The night of the accident, Angel left her friend's house after eleven o'clock and saw a light shining off the side of the road. She thought it was the headlight of a car, but when she got closer, she realized it was a motorcycle. She looked ahead of her while she was sitting in her car and saw something black in the middle of the highway. She drove up to the object, opened her car door, and saw Kelton lying in the middle of the highway with his helmet on, gasping for breath. She reported the accident and then called her mother, who was a nurse.

Angel's mother told her to block Kelton's body off with her car. Less than five minutes after she blocked Kelton's body off, a big truck appeared on the road. Angel tried to stop the driver of the truck, but the driver would not stop. She said if her car had not been there, the driver of the truck would have run over Kelton. She said she felt helpless and all she could do was pray for him until the paramedics arrived. After she told me all of that, I told her she was right where God wanted her to be, and that I told her she was not helpless because her prayer and car helped saved his life.

After we finished talking, Angel asked me if I would go with her to Kelton's room. While we were standing at his bedside, she grabbed my hand and asked me to grab Kelton's hand so she could say a prayer. Her prayer was one of the most powerful prayers I had ever heard in my life. Before Angel left the hospital, she asked for my phone number so she could keep in touch.

I visited Kelton every day I was off from work. The commute to the hospital was a one-hour drive one way. Sometimes, I wanted to throw in the towel because I felt like I was doing too much for a person who betrayed me, but I could not. I had to be an example for our son. This was my opportunity to show my son and others that you can love yourself first, forgive, and then continue to show love to someone who caused you pain. Those times when I felt like throwing in the towel, Angel, without being aware of my feelings, would text me a spiritual and encouraging message. Her timing was always perfect. She truly was like an angel on earth to me and Kelton, but the more he healed, the more she backed away.

One morning, she texted me:

*Good morning, no matter what we go through, God sees us through any circumstance. Be encouraged and stand firm on your faith. 1 Peter 5:7*

Another morning, she texted me:

*I pray you have an amazing day, that the Lord will guide and lead you in the right direction and give you peace throughout your day. I pray for a hedge of protection over you and that God will comfort you every moment with his love. I pray his presence will be placed on you so that you feel his everlasting joy.*

As the days passed after Kelton's accident, challenges with his friend and family persisted. Clay was a very close friend of Kelton. He was in our wedding and he spent a lot of time with Kelton while we were married. He was a very likable person, but it was hard for me to trust him. I used to tell Kelton that I didn't think Clay was a true friend. Clay was also close to Justine. Clay told me he was the last person Kelton was with the night of his accident until they turned in opposite directions while riding their motorcycles to go home.

For some reason, Clay had a problem with my support of Kelton during his recovery, even though Kelton's parents had asked me to be of support. He felt like I was taking over Justine's position. Clay eventually apologized for this, but in a conversation, he revealed to me that he was aware of the betrayal that was going on during my marriage.

He started talking about how Kelton would always run the streets, but he did not mention how he himself was running the streets with him. He told me about Kelton's financial obligations. He told me he was Kelton and Justine's daughter's godfather, so he was going to buy the gifts for her birthday party since Kelton would miss it. Clay told me that Kelton and Justine had been messing around for a long time, and Kelton had Justine fooled off of lies. Clay also told me that Kelton did not know what to do when I accepted the child he had with Justine because the baby was supposed to be the final straw to get a reaction out of me.

I was amused by Clay's current reaction because when Kelton was down, he had so many negative things to say about him. I believed Clay talked about Kelton because he ran out of faith, thinking that Kelton would not recover from his injury. I told him to take Kelton's accident as a warning sign, and I encouraged him to work on changing his life because it could have been him.

After the accident, Kelton's mother got his phone records to see who he talked to the night of his accident. She realized that Justine was the last person he called. She felt like Justine was at fault because she did not answer his phone call, and if she would have answered, he would have gone to her house, which was in a different direction. Kelton's mother did not want anything to do with Justine; she blamed Justine for his accident.

Justine would visit Kelton during the early part of the morning because Kelton's mother was seldomly there during that time. Justine did not want anything to do with Kelton's mother at this point either. Kelton's mother led other people to believe Kelton and I were getting back together. She would mention things to me in an effort to encourage me to rekindle my relationship with her son. I knew there was no chance of us getting back together because I knew my worth. I believed that God didn't bring me this far for me to go back to a relationship that had broken me. Most importantly, Kelton was now in a relationship with Justine.

Over time, I started getting frustrated and tired of all of the confusion coming from Kelton's mother. She wanted me to have animosity toward Justine, but I had expressed I no longer had anything against Justine. I told Kelton's mother that I felt like she became his worst enemy. I started to become cautious of my help because I didn't want to be blamed for anything that wasn't my fault. I told Kelton's mother that we were asking God to perform a miracle and it was no one's fault what happened to Kelton. I told her that everyone needed to be on one accord because God's power is in agreement. I also told her that it was time for her to let Kelton be accountable for his own actions. I expressed to his mother my thoughts about her apologizing to Justine for her comments about her, for blaming her for Kelton's accident. I also expressed how she needed to block all of the negativity out of her life. Though she did apologize, I later found out that Justine didn't accept it because she felt it wasn't genuine.

Just because you forgive someone doesn't mean they are no longer toxic. People have to change on their own time and accord. You have the choice to rebuild any type of relationship with the people you've forgiven or not. I had grown to the place where I was healed from a lot of the hurt in my life, and I began dating again. Dating was fun, but either the timing was wrong or the men seemed to be broken and opportunist. I just wanted to be the caring person that I am and be there to support my son and ex-husband.

Before Kelton's accident, I was enjoying life, traveling, and focusing on my career. I had become a licensed cosmetologist in another state a month before. I was preparing myself to travel back and forth from South Carolina to Florida to further my career, but being there to support my son was more important. Kelton and I were at a good place in our lives. Once I had let go of all the pain and forgave him, I saw the good person that everyone else saw. He once brought the child he had with Justine around me and my family without Justine, and we treated their child as family. He would also bring their child to our son's football games without Justine, and we would watch the game together.

I lost myself going through my divorce, but I was able to find out who I really was. My pain wasn't about me only but for a bigger purpose. I felt like I was going to block my blessings if I turned my back on Kelton when I knew I could help him without losing myself. I didn't have anything to lose in my life by helping him.

I viewed Kelton's accident as a test for me. I felt like God was watching me to see how I would serve Him with my second chance at life. I felt like forgiving him was preparing me for his accident. I felt like I was right where I was supposed to be. I thought about how God gave me a second chance to live and how he showed me favor when I didn't feel I deserved it. I learned to accept the things that I could not change as a pathway to restoring my peace.

When we begin to understand the amount of control we don't have over situations, we learn to let them go and ask for wisdom in its place. There is always a lesson in the pain, and being in a position where I had to support Kelton, who had betrayed me, made me realize my purpose in life was much bigger than what I even imagined. I had to be in position to support Kelton in this time, despite all the confusion and drama.

One day, I reached out to Clay because my son wanted to see his sister. I knew Clay would make Justine feel comfortable enough to meet with me, so I knew it would be good to have him help arrange the plans. Justine and I met at the park one day with the kids. My son and I walked up to Justine and her child, and my son handed Justine his sister's birthday gift. Justine said she would've invited us to the birthday party, but she hadn't had the courage to reach out to me. We sat on a bench and discussed some things while the kids spent time together. We discussed Kelton's injury, how his mother was acting toward her and its impact on her. She told me Kelton's mother was crying and excited when she found out she was pregnant and would babysit for her. His mother's behavior and demeanor toward Justine was happy and loving in the beginning but quickly turned cold after Kelton's accident.

After seeing how Justine felt, it made me reflect on my life. I realized that Kelton's mother reacted the same way when she found out that I was pregnant. As a mother, I felt sorry for Justine. Though the decisions she made to engage with my husband at the time were wrong, she was still a mother and chose to believe the lies she was told. I didn't feel as though I owed Justine anything, but I also didn't feel like a victim either. We all have to live with our decisions and choices no matter what, and I realized the pain she was experiencing was enough. I told her I would keep her informed about the status of Kelton for the sake of their child because neither she nor her child had a voice in the situation. Justine thanked me for the help I offered.

One day, I called Justine and told her that I was going to back away—I was at my peaceful place in life, and I knew she had to get to hers—but she could call me if she needed me. I realized that even with my efforts, I couldn't stand in the way of Justine's own revelations. Just like I had, she would have to learn the hard way about Kelton. I realized she probably was shocked by how all the promises Kelton made to her turned out not only to be untrue but ultimately resulted in her not being accepted by his family. We both realized that Kelton omitted a lot of details about his co-parenting relationship with me. Kelton's accident exposed a lot of lies and truths.

## #LessonLearned

People will paint a picture for you that they want you to believe, even if it's not true. When we don't trust or truly value ourselves, we choose not to ask questions or truly dig into what others tell us; we believe what we want to believe instead. People's behaviors, when not given time to be corrected, ultimately repeat themselves and that is why it's important to not just listen to what a person says but to observe what they do consistently. Forgiving another person's past doesn't mean you shouldn't be cautious as you proceed forward.

## #WorthTheCost

I do not know why Kelton's accident happened. But I do know that meeting and spending time with Angel revealed the peace of God that is always surrounding us, even in the midst of our storm and our shortcomings. The grace that came our way and spared Kelton's life gave me an opportunity to confront one of the women who I felt participated in the destruction of my home, and put me in a position to practice grace and true forgiveness despite (but not in place of) my feelings.

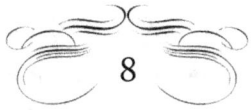

# The Power of God's Grace and Mercy

Imagine if you were to handle your challenges and storms your way instead of God's way. Imagine where your life would be if it had not been for God's grace and mercy. Imagine where your life would be if you were to give up on your faith.

After Kelton was discharged from the hospital, he was transported to a nursing facility. The commute to the nursing facility was a two-hour drive one way. In the nursing facility, he was awake and breathing on his own, but he could not talk or follow commands. One day, I was sitting in his room watching his body movement, or what his doctor in the hospital had called "reflexes" when Kelton was unconscious. This time, I didn't believe his body movements were reflexes like the doctor said they were. I saw something deeper. I reflected back on how Kelton communicated with me through his body language during our marriage. I saw the power of God taking over his body! I sat on a chair at the side of his bed and watched his left arm move rapidly from side to side like he was throwing punches, his left leg moving like he was stomping and the right side of his body was still with his right hand contracting to the middle of his chest. Then I reflected on these two Bible verses:

> *"And the God of peace shall bruise Satan under your feet shortly. The grace of our Lord Jesus Christ be with you. Amen."*
> Romans 16:20

> *"For I the Lord thy God will hold thy right hand, saying unto thee, Fear not; I will help thee."*
> Isaiah 41:13

I felt like God was using Kelton's body to tell me to be still and not to lose faith and allow Him to order my steps because He was helping Kelton fight his storm and crushing Satan under His feet while He was holding Kelton's right hand. Once I realized this, I kept my faith and started motivating Kelton spiritually, mentally, and physically every time I visited him.

One day, I told Kelton that I needed him to start following commands because I was trying to help him. His speech therapist came in later on that day with an update.

She told me and his mother he would drink out of a straw but would not follow commands. She went and got a cup of water and a straw. He drank some of the water from the straw. Then, she told him to touch his nose. He slowly lifted his left arm and touched his nose. Me and Kelton's mother said, "Thank you, Jesus" at the same time. She asked him to stick his tongue out, and he did it with the little strength he had. His speech therapist was shocked!

I went back to visit him another day and told him I needed for him to start talking, so he could start making his own decisions. A few weeks later, I took my son to visit him for the first time since his accident. It had been five months since he had seen his father, and he told me he wanted to spend part of his spring break with him. I had to prepare my son in advance for this moment because he was not ready to see his father, and I did not want to pressure him. My son and I would pray together for his father. I would show him pictures and videos of Kelton while educating him on his progress.

I am glad I did not hold anything back about Kelton's condition because my son went to school one day and a child picked on him about his father's condition. The child told my son, that is why your daddy can't walk or talk. What the child said bothered my son, but he was able to brush it off. My son came to me one night after he took his bath and said, "Mama, I listen to three gospel songs on my cell phone before I get out of the tub." I realized my son was using music to help heal, which was the same thing I did after finding out I was betrayed. I learned that during my healing, I was actually teaching my son a way to heal. My son handled his first visit with a lot of strength. Before we were getting ready to leave, I wanted to make sure Kelton was still following commands. I asked Kelton to give our son a pound, and he did.

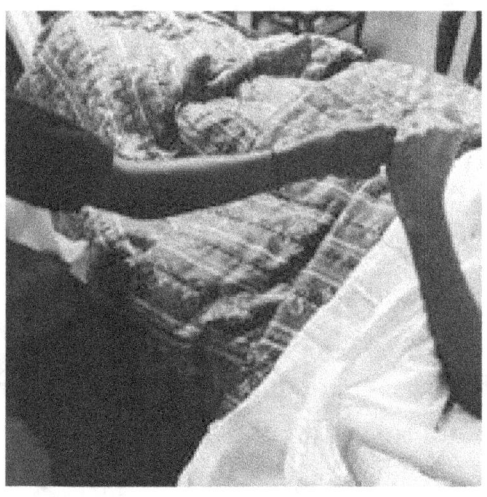

*My son and his father giving each other a pound*

A couple weeks later, I took my son and my nephew to visit Kelton. I asked Kelton who I was, and he whispered, "Candace." Then, I asked him, did he know our son and my nephew? He whispered our son's name and my nephew's nickname.

Later on that day, Kelton was moving like something was bothering him. I asked him what was wrong, and he wouldn't say, but he kept moving. Then, he whispered to me, asking if he could have a hug. Most of the time, a hug is a gesture people use to say hello or goodbye. I did not know where his mind would have gone once he got a hug from me, but I knew he would fight hard for what he could not have. I told him not today and to keep fighting!

During another visit, while I was sitting in the sunroom with my son, niece, and nephew, I noticed Kelton pulling on the sheet that was covering his body from his neck to his feet. He started pulling on the sheet every time he felt it falling down. The way he was pulling on the sheet made me feel like he didn't want anyone to see him because of his contracted body parts. I began to ask him questions to see how much progress he had made from his brain injury.

I asked him, "Where are you?"

He replied, "At the hospital."

"Why are you here?"

"Motorcycle accident."

"What did you hurt?"

"My leg, arm, and pride."

After he said all of that, I stimulated his mind spiritually. I told him it is important to have a relationship with God and that he had to pray for what he wanted God to do for him.

I asked him, "What do you want God to do for you?"

He replied, "Help me." Then he took a pause and said, "God, help me."

The next day, I was at work styling my client's hair. I asked the young lady to tell me her plans after she graduated from high school. She said she wanted to be a motivational speaker. My client is paralyzed, and some of her body parts are contracted. I began to tell her Kelton's story. After I told her his story and showed her a picture of what his accident did to him, she asked me if she could go visit and talk to him one day because she knew how it felt to be looked at differently. I told her yes. She looked at me with a look of excitement and replied, "I never thought I would be able to be a motivational speaker!"

After Kelton started talking, Clay called me for an update on how Kelton was doing. During our conversation, I asked him about Justine, and he told me Justine had moved. I was shocked that she had moved away with Kelton's child without him knowing. I told Clay that I believed Justine waited for us to get a divorce to have a child by him and moved away because things did not turn out the way she expected. She had been waiting around on him all this time, so why couldn't she wait for him to heal? He said she had already been planning to move. I told Clay, "So you let Justine take your godchild and leave Kelton for dead! Where was your voice? You thought I was taking over, blocking Justine from being there for Kelton, and she left him on his bed of affliction."

A week after I talked to Clay, Justine called me. She told me she knew it was strange for her to call because it had been a while since we talked. Though she said it wasn't the reason, I felt the reason she was calling was because of Clay sharing what I said to him. In my healing process, I had realized that holding on to grudges or withholding the truth would never benefit me.

I told Justine everything I told Clay about her and to be mindful of him. She told me she felt comfortable enough to talk to me about her situation. Kelton had painted a perfect picture of their future life together, and she had believed they would be a happy family. Justine knew she had to forgive Kelton's mother, but she wasn't sure how to so that her child could have a relationship with Kelton's family. I told her about my own journey of forgiveness, and that, for her own sanity, she should forgive his mother and let her build her trust back with her.

Justine told me she had to take a month off of work and go to counseling after Kelton's accident because she could not handle what life had thrown at her. She had just given birth to their child months before Kelton's accident.

He missed their child's first Christmas and birthday. She transferred her job and had taken a pay cut and sold her house to move in to an apartment so she could be closer to Kelton. She made all of those sacrifices, and less than a year later, Kelton suffered from a brain injury. She told me she moved to another state so she could find herself, but her loyalty was still with Kelton and she would still come to see him. I made it clear to her that I did not have any hard feelings toward her in spite of everything, and I wished them well in life.

After my conversation with Justine, I began to think, somewhat ironically, about how important it is to be mindful of the things we do and the people we take for granted. During the time Kelton and I were married, I tried to help him save money by switching his motorcycle insurance, and as a result of that, it led me to his betrayal and he later ended up in a bad motorcycle accident. I never imagined that I would have to watch Kelton fight for his life after he watched me fight for mine. He left our marriage for a woman who left him on his bed of affliction. I felt tortured for seventeen months going through my divorce with him and his doctor prognosis that his brain injury would take twelve to eighteen months or longer to heal.

Three weeks before his accident, Kelton had started a new job at a nursing facility. He had told my father that if something were to happen to him, he was not to let anyone put him in the nursing facility he worked at. I feel like that was the reason he kept my father close to him. Two months before Kelton's accident, I received flowers at work from an anonymous sender. I thought one of the guys I went on a date with sent them, but a few weeks after I received the flowers, my father told my youngest sister that Kelton had sent the flowers to me. I didn't mention anything to Kelton about the flowers after I found out he sent them. In hindsight, I think Kelton sent the flowers to thank me in advance for taking care of him after his accident.

The next time I visited Kelton, when I was getting ready to leave, I told him to take care.

He whispered, "What does that mean?"

"Don't give up."

"Don't leave me."

The thought ran through my head: would it be fair for me to stop living my life because of the life he chose to live? I do not care how much you motivate a person in life; it is up to them to use everything that God has already imparted to them to get out of their storms. I knew if I were still married to him, I would have tried to see if I could have taken care of him at home.

Leaving Kelton in an environment where he did not want to be was just as hard as it was for me to heal from a divorce after being betrayed by him. I had to pray and ask God to reveal to me what else that I could do for Kelton. I felt like I did my best at helping him with the boundaries of our co-parenting relationship. At this point, he had short and long-term memory loss and mobility issues. He would talk normally and then talk as if he was talking in his sleep and he would forget he was in a motorcycle accident. He thought he was in a hospital instead of a nursing facility. Sometimes, the memory that he had left led him to believe that his deceased grandparent was still living and that we were still married. I felt like he was blocking out painful moments in his life because of his hurt pride.

A year after Kelton's motorcycle accident, exactly one week before Christmas in 2017, my brother was in a car accident. My brother had just gotten off from working a twelve-hour shift. He was thirteen minutes away from home and fell asleep behind the wheel of his truck. He hit a tree going sixty miles per hour and walked away from his accident with a small scratch on his knee and a little soreness in his chest from the impact of the airbag. The state trooper sympathized with my brother and didn't give him any traffic violation tickets.

The same week of my brother's accident, two of my clients told me that if they would've left from their destination a few minutes earlier, they would've witnessed my brother's accident or he could've hit their cars. I thanked God for His covering and thought to myself, with tears running down my face, if I would've continued living my life with an angry, bitter, and unforgiving heart toward my ex-husband, would the outcome of my brother's accident been the same? I felt like my brother's accident was God's way of telling me to get some rest.

I know who I am, I know what I've done, and I know where I've been, but God still chose to love me, forgive me, and wake me up! I give God my best praise—hallelujah! I thank God for showing me GMC in my life—grace, mercy, and comfort!

---

### #LessonLearned

Everyone has pain, a story of brokenness, and a need to learn to value and love themselves more. I learned that seeking revenge because of my past hurt would not have been worth the cost of me completely losing myself, a family member, or client.

---

## #WorthTheCost

The purpose of my storm with Kelton was for me to find out who I really was. Once I reached my peaceful place in life, I realized that those seventeen months of torture happened to teach me invaluable lessons. It was worth learning I do not have to settle in life. It was worth learning to love myself first. It was worth learning to always be there for my son and that we could make it on our own, just the two of us. It was worth learning how to love and forgive. It was worth learning how to let go of anything weighing me down. It was worth learning I cannot control anyone but me. I do not have to be afraid to give my heart away fully because I learned my worth! It was worth learning I cannot make it in life without a relationship with God. It was worth learning that when I feel a divine pull on my heart by God for me to move, then that is when I should move. Most importantly, it was worth learning that God will give me a warning sign before He does anything, but it is up to me to see it!

# 9

# I Am Restored with Peace

Today, are you willing to trust God with your challenges or past hurts? Are you willing to forgive yourself and others and keep your faith in order to gain freedom and peace?

Today, I am at a peaceful place in life, but before I got here, I had to forgive myself and everyone who needed my forgiveness, regardless if they were sorry or not. I have never experienced a view as beautiful as this place in my life! My peaceful place made me view my storms on a godly level. I am not perfect and I will not claim to be, but when God was in the midst of my storms, I got through them easier. My peaceful place in life had me doing things that I knew only God would be able to make me do! I am better spiritually, I am wealthier with wisdom, and I am stronger than ever!

I will not expect more out of someone else than what I expect out of myself. I will not take anything or anyone for granted. I will always remain humble because going back to ground zero can happen in a matter of seconds. I realize that every situation in my life is a test for me, so I will find my purpose in it. I will forever be thankful for my family and friends who are always there to pray for me and help me when my back is against the wall.

I am living the rest of my life knowing some of the same people I go hard for will not go hard for me. I am living the rest of my life knowing it is okay to be hurt because strength and character are built from it. I am living the rest of my life knowing I do not have to show people who they are because someone else will. I am living the rest of my life spreading my blessings because I know nothing good comes to a selfish person.

I understand everybody who started with me on my journey will not finish with me because you have to learn what type of people you are supposed to be around. I realize it is better to be talked about than to be around people who love to talk. It is also better to stand alone than to stand with people who will fall for anything. I have realized that it is easy to be judged by others when they do not understand. Most importantly, I have realized that being a good person in a peaceful place in life can change a lot of things!

I have been in remission for nine years. I have been self-employed for eleven years. I am currently working ten days a month, less than forty hours a week, and my cup is running over with prosperity. I became a godmother for the first time to a beautiful little girl. I purchased some land just in case I ever decide to open my own salon one day or use it as an investment toward my son's future.

It has been an emotional journey for me and my son. A journey that required a lot of dedication, time, tears, love, support, and most importantly, prayer. My son and I have a close relationship. He became very protective of me after his experience with the divorce and his father's accident. I couldn't ask for a better child. He's very respectful, happy, and helpful, and he is doing well in school. He has adjusted to our new lifestyle without his father living with us, and he cherishes every moment that he has to show his father love and support. I am unaware if Justine's loyalty is still with Kelton, but my son has adjusted to his sister moving away, and I believe, in God's perfect timing, that he will gain a stable relationship with his sister.

I spend most of my spare time hanging out with my family and friends and traveling. I'm at the place in my life where if you break my heart once, you won't break it twice! I'm dating but waiting on God to send me the man who is meant for me. God is definitely in my heart, and I have introduced my son to Him. I am so appreciative and thankful for life. I try to treat everyone fairly and with kindness because God kept me here when He could have easily taken my life. Every situation that I encounter in my life, I evaluate it first. I ask myself, is it worth me fighting or worth

God defending me? Meaning, is it better for me to not focus on trying to win over a situation with my own power but to trust that God will sort it out with little effort from me. I have learned that every battle in my life is not mine but the Lord's. I pray every day for God to continue covering my health and my family.

I'm peacefully enjoying life, walking with faith and confidence, and focusing on furthering my career. I can honestly say I am in love with the restored Candace! I will not die trying to be loyal to my past but only my future. I would rather leave this world with growth than live in it sleeping and not truly enjoying it.

### #LessonLearned

Don't bury your opportunity to restore your peace.

### #WorthTheCost

I have so much comfort in knowing that God knows everything and that He has the whole world in his hands. Put God first in everything you do and give thanks through the good and bad times. Faith without work is dead! Always remember, all things are possible only if you believe!

# Restoring Your Peace

My journey has been one that has made me confront my insecurities and demons and helped me realize that peace is truly important. For you reading this, I hope my story has helped you identify areas in your life where you may be operating outside of your own peace and need healing. If that is the case, I offer the formula below, which helps me reconnect to myself when life is stressful.

The formula for restoring your peace during challenges:

(Your Name x Believe) + (Faith x Size of Mustard Seed) = PEACE

The formula for restoring your peace after storms:

(Your Name x Believe) + Own Your Truth + Forgiveness + (Faith x Size of Mustard Seed) = PEACE

# Thank You

I would like to humbly thank God, who is the head of my life. God, thank you for being my strength in my times of weakness. Thank you for being my healer. Thank you for keeping and forgiving me. God, thank you for the biggest blessing that changed my life—my son. Thank you for my truth, my growth and my peace. God, thank you for seeking my heart. Most importantly, thank you for my God-given purpose.

To my parents, Levon and Christine Patrick, thank you for introducing me to God. Thank you for my wings and allowing me to fly on my own. Thank you for my siblings (Christina, Krystal, Levon, and Jeremy) who keep life interesting. There has never been a dull or silent moment in the presence of them and their children. Most importantly, thank you for your love and faith.

To my brother-in-law, Mike, thank you for risking your life for our country. Thank you for all that you've done and for everything I know you'll do. Thank you for being yourself around me and the many jokes that you love to tell. You're an amazing bonus brother!

A special thank you to my sixteen-year-old niece, Madison. Thank you for dedicating your time and effort drawing the portrait of me, that is found on the cover of this book. I pray that you will reach your highest potential as a future artist.

To the reader of this book, thank you so much for your support. I will not take it for granted.

# About the Author

Candace Patrick is a licensed cosmetologist and cancer survivor who believes her purpose is to touch more hearts than hair. Her mission is to use the lessons she has learned to help others get through their storms in life.

Candace earned her bachelor of science in math and computer science from the University of South Carolina Aiken. She currently resides in Blackville, South Carolina, with her son. In her spare time, she enjoys hanging out with her family and friends and traveling.

To connect, visit her Facebook at Candace Patrick or Instagram @Stylist_81

If this book has made a difference in your life, please consider leaving a review on Amazon.

www.ingramcontent.com/pod-product-compliance
Lightning Source LLC
Chambersburg PA
CBHW072101290426
44110CB00014B/1768